T0198902

Jamie Noraa
The Inspired Dreamer

Written by Gregory Harris,
Illustrated by Cecillia Wilber

AuthorHouse™
1663 Liberty Drive
Bloomington, IN 47403
www.authorhouse.com
Phone: 833-262-8899

This book is printed on acid-free paper.

ISBN: 978-1-4490-6310-8 (sc)

Library of Congress Control Number: 2009914000

Print information available on the last page.

Published by AuthorHouse 06/17/2021

authorHOUSE®

I would like to dedicate this book to the wonderful teachers I had in grade school. One of my favorite teachers was my fifth grade teacher at Harris Elementary, located in North Little Rock in the Pulaski County School District. The Late Beatrice Lewis, allowed me to write plays and use the students in the classroom as actors and actresses to present my skits to the entire classroom.

I would also like to thank my parents for their love and support down through the years. My father purchased my first organ when I was around twelve years old and this is where I developed my passion for writing stories and songs.

I hope this book will inspire children and adults everywhere to dream big because the sky is the limit to what you can achieve if you are willing to work hard and go after your dreams.

Once upon a time there was a boy named Jamie Noraa. Jamie had three brothers, Jimmy, Johnny, and James, and three sisters, Minnie, Marcy, and Monica. Jamie loved the simple things in life such as going to school, playing with his brothers and sisters, visiting his grandparents during the summer months when school was closed for summer break, and sleeping when it rained.

Jamie had wonderful parents who loved and cared about him and his brothers and sisters. His father Daniel worked at the local bank as teller and his mother Loretta worked at the community bakery. The Noraa family was a very close knit family who worked together and always showed love to each other.

The parents gathered the family together monthly to talk about family and community issues. One day, during a family meeting, Jamie's father talked to the family about being the very best that they could be and always shooting for the stars, never settling for anything less. Then he asked the children a question, "Have you ever dreamed about something that you wished would come true?" All of the children looked puzzled except Jamie, because he loved to sleep and dream while the rain bounced upon his bedroom windows.

Jamie's father said, "When I was young, I used to dream about working in a bank, counting large sums of money, and greeting customers as they rushed into the bank a second before the bank closed." Then he said, "I can remember telling my parents about those dreams. My mother would often tell me, "Son, hold your head up and keep on dreaming because dreams can come true." When it was time for everyone to speak, each child got a chance to speak. All the brothers and sisters were older than Jamie, so they always beat him to the punch. They spoke first, and when it was his turn to speak, Jamie closed his eyes and began to think about the rain and his dreams that he had dreamed. On this particular day they came alive within the corners of his mind.

Jamie said, "I can remember one day when I visited Grandma Winnie and Grandpa Walter. We were sitting at the kitchen table eating away on the delicious meal that Grandma had prepared. We were helping ourselves to Grandma's down home cooking of Southern fried chicken, corn on the cob, greens, beans, tomatoes, sweet potatoes, and buttermilk cornbread. For dessert, we had home- made ice-cream and sour cream pound cake. I ate until I thought my stomach was going to pop open. After dinner I helped Grandma clean off the table, wash the dishes, take out the trash, sweep the kitchen floor, and put the left-over food into the refrigerator.

Then, I watched television with Grandpa Walter. He loved to watch the Evening News. Finally, it was time for me to get ready for bed. All of the sudden, I heard the thunder roar and the rain started falling from the opened sky. It sounded like a pack of wild horses running to get away from capture. As soon as I finished my bath, I said my prayers and jumped into the soft and cozy bed that Grandma Winnie had prepared for me.

As the rain continued bouncing on my window pane, it made a musical sound like drip drop, drip drop, drip, drip, drip drop and splash, splash, splash. Before I knew it, I was fast asleep and I began to dream. I dreamed that I was on a stage singing a delightful song before thousands and thousands of people. There were so many people that I couldn't even count them if I had wanted to. I was front and center up on a big stage. All of the attention was pointed towards me as I sang a delightful song for the people who listened. After I finished singing my song, I knew that the people loved it because they immediately jumped out of their seats and began to shout and clap their hands as if to say, "Our souls are satisfied and we applaud you for your efforts."

Jamie's mother Loretta said, "That's a wonderful dream Jamie, hold your head up and keep on dreaming because dreams can come true."

At last it was time for the family to end its monthly meeting. They stood up and gave each other a big hug. Jamie's father said, "Let's go to the movie theater to watch one of the hit movies." They dressed and got into the family van that was parked in the garage. As they arrived at the movie theater, the dad and mom held hands and softly laughed. Jamie really admired the closeness of his mom and dad. His dad always worked hard so that his family could have the best. Sometimes he worked three or four small jobs so that the family could survive.

When the family made it to the cashier's booth, Mr. Noraa pulled a twenty-dollar bill from this pocket. The cost of the movie tickets was three-dollars for adults, one dollar for kids six and under, and two dollars for kids over twelve. The total cost for the family was nineteen dollars. Jamie's parents paid three dollars each. Jimmy, Johnny, Jackie, Minnie, Marcy, and Martha paid two dollars each. Since Jamie was six years old, his cost was only one dollar. Mr. Noraa gave the cashier the twenty dollar bill, and she gave him a receipt and his one dollar bill change.

The family moved quickly to the refreshment stand where there was popcorn, candy, hot dogs, nachos and cheese dip, cold drinks, and frozen Icy. Mr. Noraa purchased three large bags of popcorn and nine large drinks. The popcorn was fresh and buttery, and the drinks were ice cold. When Jamie held his drink in his hands, it felt just like the cold rain falling upon his head as he ran from the school bus into his school's cafeteria on a bright winter day. When they opened the door to the movie theater room it was dark and light in places. The room was nearly full, but there were just enough seats for the family to in the front, close to the movie screen. As soon as they sat down, the movie previews began showing commercials and upcoming community events. Jamie's dad chose a family oriented movie. The movie was about a family who won a free trip to Hawaii. After arriving in Hawaii, the family checked into a grand hotel. They also had an opportunity to snorkel, and explore the deep blue sea. The family was given 10,000 dollars for spending money.

The movie was excellent and everyone stayed awake, except Jamie who was too busy dreaming. When he awoke, Jamie shared his dream with his brothers and sisters. He told them that he dreamed of standing on a big stage with a famous singer performing a duet which made the audience jump out of their seats with shouts of joy. The song went something like this: "Deep Blue Sea, Deep Blue Sea, Everybody loves to explore the Deep Blue sea." The family stopped by the rest-rooms before walking to their van, and Jamie's dad drove them home.

When they arrived home, they went to their bedrooms and began to get ready for bed. The parents came into the boys' room and said, "Goodnight boys." Then they left the room and walked to the sisters' room. After they turned off all of the lights, it didn't take long for Jamie to fall asleep. It had been a long day and he was very tired.

The next day was Monday and the family awoke early. Jamie could smell the breakfast that his mother was cooking. It smelled like crispy bacon, homemade buttermilk biscuits, scrambled eggs, and rice. Mr. Noraa said, "Boys, it's time to get up. Today is the first day of school." Jamie was so excited. His brothers and sisters were already in school, but this was Jamie's very first day of elementary school. All of the children got up and made their beds. One by one they raced to see who would be the next one to make it to the bathroom to get ready for the brand new school year. As soon as they were dressed and ready, they hurried down to the kitchen table to eat breakfast. Mrs. Noraa said, "You better hurry because your dad and I will drop you off before it's time for us to go to our jobs."

They dropped the older sisters and brothers off first, and then they dropped Jamie off at the new elementary school that was about a block from their house. After they parked the car, Jamie and his parents walked to the main office. They met the school secretary who greeted them with a warm smile and welcome. Jamie's parents walked him to his classroom. The teacher's name was printed on the door. It read Ms. Sylvia Lewis, First Grade. The door was opened by a lady with a warm smile who shook hands, and said, "What is your son's name?" Mr. Noraa said, "His name is Jamie Noraa "The teacher said, "Oh what a wonderful name."

As Jamie entered the classroom, the teacher escorted him to his desk. On the right hand side of the room was a large piano and in the back of the room was a reading loft. The teacher asked each student to tell about something they had done during summer months. When it was Jamie's turn, he told them about the night when he visited his grandparents, went to sleep, and had a dream. He told them that he dreamed that he was singing on a big stage before thousands and thousands of people. Jamie's teacher said to the class, "Very good. Students, hold your heads up and dream, dream, dream, because your dreams can come true." Then she walked over to the piano and said, "I'm going to teach you a brand new song. The name of this song is "Dream, Dream, Dream," and it goes something like this." She began to sing, 1-2-3 Dream, Dream, Dream 1-2-3 Dream, Dream, Dream, 1-2-3 Dream, Dream, Dream every times it rains Drip Drop, Drip Drop, Drip Drop Dream, Dream, Dream every time it rains. First she taught the girls their parts and then she taught the boys their parts. Then she had all of the students join together to sing the song "Dream, Dream, Dream." She told the students what they would be doing that day. Then she called them by rows to sit on the carpet in the back of the room for story time. She read a story about the inspired dreamer.

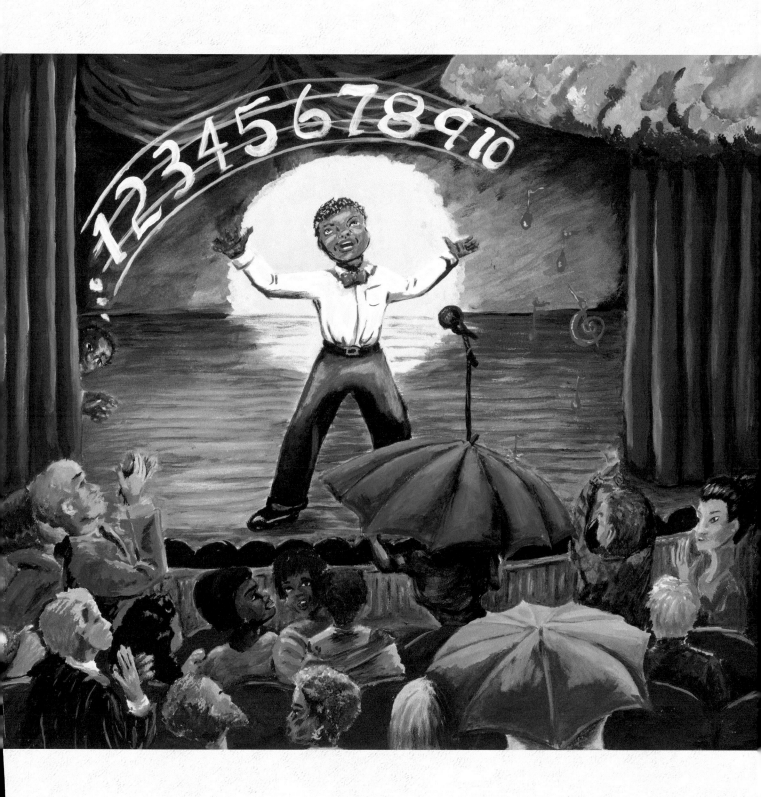

Author Bio

Greg Harris is a educator, singer, and song writer. Greg is a Sabbath Day Records Gospel Recording Artist. Greg is a formal teacher with the Little Rock School District located in Little Rock, Arkansas. Greg is currently working for the Des Moines Education Association in Des Moines, Iowa as Executive Director. Greg works with teachers, associates and clerical workers in advocating for children and public education. Greg started singing professional in 1986. Greg's first record title "Songs From The Heart received regional and national success. His current record "Minster Greg Harris Live In Little Rock is currently being promoted nationally. He started writing this book in 2007 when he worked in Charlotte, North Carolina with the North Carolina Association of Educators. Greg received is undergraduate degree from Arkansas, Baptist College in Little Rock, Arkansas and his graduate's degree from The University Of Central Arkansas (UCA.)

Illustrator Bio

Cecillia Wilber is a mother of 4 and has 11 grandchildren. She currently works for the Des Moines Public School District located in Des Moines, Iowa. For the past 17 years she has enjoyed working in the classroom with challenging students and she loves when she sees improvements from her efforts with students.

She's been involved with doing a lot of artwork for the schools such as creating sceneries for plays and designing T-shirts. She has always had a passion for artwork and at an early age dreamed of working for Walt Disney. Cecillia says "after reading Greg's manuscript of his story she was able to transmit the pictures that came to mind to create illustrations that breathed colors of life into the book".

Printed in the United States
by Baker & Taylor Publisher Services